WOW!
Stories from Real Life
A Low-Beginning, Multi-Skills Text

Natalie Hess • Laurel Pollard

Alta Book Center
PUBLISHERS

Acquisitions Editor: Aaron Almendares-Berman
Editor: Jamie Ann Cross
Cover Design and Interior Illustrations: Andrew Lange Illustration
Interior Design and Page Layout: Emily Wright

Photograph Credits
The publisher thanks Geneva and Terry for bringing several stories in this book to life via their photography:
Geneva Hickey (*Maria Finds a Friend, The Translator, Living in the Library, Alex and Beth*)
Terry Coleman (*The 75-Year Friendship, Meeting the New Neighbor*)

The publisher wishes to extend special thanks to the following persons for their help and assistance in providing
photographs for *Eduardo Saves a Home*, the story that takes place in Brazil:

Rogério Rodrigues
Photographer
Instituto Dois Irmãos
Rio de Janeiro-RJ, Brazil

Daniela A. Myer
Academic Consultant
Cambridge University Press
Rio de Janeiro-RJ, Brazil

The publisher wishes to acknowledge with appreciation Susan and Neil Silverman, photographers at
www.thesilvermansphotography.com, for their assistance and guidance with the photograph for *Eduardo Saves a Home*.

A final thank you to Madeleine Halvarsson for her permission to use the photo in *Lost and Found*.

Alta Book Center Publishers
Post Office Box 1736
Provo, Utah 84603 USA

Tel: 800 ALTA/ESL (Mexico, Canada and USA)
Other International: 801.377.1530
Fax: 800 ALTA/FAX
International: 801.222.9199
Email: info@altaesl.com • Website: www.altaesl.com

ISBN: 978-1-932383-14-0
Library of Congress Control Number: 2008925905

Contents

Answer Key
> For a complete answer key (downloadable for free)
> visit www.altaesl.com.

Dedication

We dedicate this book to the memory of Jean Zukowski/Faust—
our mentor, colleague, and friend.

Acknowledgements

Our Inspirers: hard-working teachers of low-beginning classes.

Our Instigators: Aaron Almendares-Berman and Simon Almendares-Berman of
Alta Book Center Publishers.

Our Sources: The real people who lived the 5,000 stories we read and heard as we were
choosing the eight stories in this book.

Our Choosers: Hundreds of ESL students—teens and adults, men and women, from various
countries of origin—who voted on dozens of stories. We analyzed your votes, and here are the stories
you liked the best.

Our Focus Group Teachers: Adele Youmans, Mary Carol Wagner, Lois Miller, Masha Gromyko,
Jennifer Esh, Barbara Birdsall, and Paula Cortes. You showed us what you want in a real
low-beginning book for teens and adults. We cannot thank you enough for your generosity,
thoughtfulness, and commitment.

Our Reviewers: Sandy Briggs and Rick Kappra. You helped us make this book much better!

Our Field Testers: Libby Swanson and Elizabeth Goodwin. You took these materials into your
classrooms. We're glad you and your students liked them! Thank you for your valuable advice.

Our Content Editor: Paula Schlusberg, always helpful and thoroughly professional.

Fabulous photos: Terry Coleman

More fabulous photos, data entry, and good ideas: Geneva Hickey

Field test analyses, computer troubleshooting, cover ideas, and good hot soup: Dan Blanco

Cheerful chauffeuring and support: John Hess

Cross-cultural sensitivity monitor: Lauren McElroy

We owe a great deal to those who have taught us, including the writers of books we have used as
teachers. The book in your hands holds our best thinking. We know future writers will add more to
the collective, creative sea we are all swimming in as we all do our best for our students.

*A special thanks to our creative, patient, watchful editor, Jamie Cross; our designer Emily Wright; and to all
the helpful folks at Alta.*

Introduction I *(At-a-Glance)*

Welcome to *Wow! Stories from Real Life*

You'll notice that the student pages look very simple, as they must for low-beginning students. But there is so much you can do with every page!

Just take a look at the *Notes to the Teacher* in the back of the book, page 137. Here is a quote from one of our field-testing teachers:

> "Sometimes I thought my students wouldn't need every step in the *Notes to the Teacher*. But I followed the recommended sequence, and my students loved it! They also remembered what they'd learned. I think I've been moving too fast, not giving them time to really learn. **This book is helping me become a better teacher.**"
>
> – Libby Swanson, Eastside Learning Center, Tucson, Arizona

Very soon, you won't need to refer to the *Notes to the Teacher* any more. You and your students will know these teaching routines like the back of your hand!

Your low-beginning students need:
- plenty of direct teaching,
- frequent changes of activity,
- frequent monitoring, and
- a lot of help from you along the way.

This book will make all of this easier. The activities in this book:
- engage each student at his or her own level,
- get even your low-beginning students interacting and learning independently,
- give your students instant feedback on correctness, and
- **provide teaching routines that require little or no preparation time by you.**

Wow! Stories from Real Life is the book you've been waiting for. Reading *Introduction II* and the *Notes to the Teacher* will help you get the full benefits of each exercise.

Our aim: to make the rest of your teaching life easier, more successful, and more fun!

Introduction II (*Detailed*)

Important! For specific notes on teaching each exercise, see *Notes to the Teacher* on page 137.

How *Wow!* is Organized

Wow! Stories from Real Life has eight units, each focused on a true story. The stories are written in the present tense. (You will find additional exercises using the simple past in our online resources. See page 8 for more information.)

The exercises include:
- extensive pre-reading;
- rich activities for comprehension, vocabulary, and holistic grammar; and
- personalized extensions that even very low-beginning students can handle.

The exercises progress from more controlled to more free within each unit.

More than a reader, *Wow!* will help your students' language expand in every way!

The Real-Life Stories

Everyone loves a good story! *Wow!* unfolds heart-warming stories of reuniting families, of people in (and out of) love, and of unusual homes (see *Living in the Library*). Addressing personal themes encourages students to recall, talk, and write about their own experiences.

These stories really happened. They are all taken from the news or from personal experiences of students we know. We will never forget the against-all-odds reunion of Elizabeth and her brother Charles, which happened in Tucson, Arizona (see *Meeting the New Neighbor*).

Students love these eight stories because:
- they are **true**,
- they are **upbeat**,
- they are **surprising**, and
- they are related to **universal human experience**.

When students are eager to read, their best learning strategies are activated; good stories wake up the brain!

How did we select these particular stories? We read over 5,000 stories and chose twenty-five that:
- interested us most and
- used vocabulary beginning students need.

Then we asked hundreds of teen and adult immigrant students to rank the twenty-five stories for us. *Wow!* is a collection of the eight stories they liked best!

Wow! and Progressive Cloze Exercises

Wow! uniquely features *Progressive Cloze* exercises. (We call them *Fill in the Blanks* in the book.) Research shows that cloze is an excellent holistic exercise. Cloze is powerful and easy to use. Students learn grammar, spelling, and vocabulary all together, in context.

Cloze exercises:
- provide a great deal of independent work;
- let students work at their own pace;
- can be done individually or collaboratively;
- are excellent in multi-level classes—more advanced students are challenged, and slower students don't feel overwhelmed; and
- are good assessment tools (students' scores on comprehensive language exams correlate well to their scores on one single section of those exams: the cloze section).

The *Progressive Cloze* exercises in *Wow!* take cloze to the next level. The progressive cloze sequence builds students' confidence via the following steps: students try a cloze, correct it immediately, and then try it again. They repeat this with three progressively more challenging cloze versions of the story. Students are surprised at how much they can do; they are especially surprised that what looked like a daunting set of blank spaces has quickly become a task that's within their power!

Teachers who field-tested these materials reported that *Progressive Cloze* has become one of their favorite teaching routines. It keeps students engaged while the teacher is out of the spotlight, enabling the teacher to think, assist students, or simply breathe.

Wow! and Built-in Assessment

For administrators:
Funding and student advancement often depend on provable results. The exercises in this book can be collected as needed as proofs of student progress. In particular, the Progressive Cloze exercises (*Fill in the Blanks*) at the end of each unit provide reliable, valid assessment.

For teachers:
As a teacher, you need regular feedback to make informed decisions about what to review, when to recycle, when to introduce new material, and who needs extra help. However, most teachers don't have time to make and grade a lot of quizzes—and students find quizzes threatening. It is far better to have assessment built into the exercises—*Wow!* has done that work for you!

For students:
Students need regular feedback too. Your students will immediately check their own answers in this book. When they see their progress, they stay motivated and excited about learning. The innovative Progressive Cloze exercises (*Fill in the Blanks*) are especially fun!

Wow! and a Suggested Time Framework

Teachers who field-tested this book—and fully used the exercises and teaching suggestions— found that each unit engaged students for about 5 hours. You and your students may need more time—or less.

Wow! and Multi-level Classes

Wow! Stories from Real Life offers great flexibility:
- you can pick and choose from a rich menu of exercises and teaching suggestions (see the *Notes to the Teacher,* page 137); and
- your students can work individually, in pairs, or in groups, enabling them to do many of the exercises at their own pace.

Answer Key

An answer key is available online (downloadable for free). Go to www.altaesl.com and search for the keyword: *Wow!*

Online Resources

Go to www.altaesl.com and search for the keyword: *Wow!* to discover more resources and suggestions for using them.

The online site includes:
- captionless pictures for all the stories
- more great strategies for using these pictures
- all eight stories in the simple past tense
- engaging exercises to practice simple past verbs
- verb lists—present and past forms of the verbs in each story
- more vocabulary exercises

Contact the Authors

We hope you and your students enjoy this book. Please write to us with your questions and suggestions. We welcome your feedback.

Natalie Hess
http://jan.ucc.nau.edu/nbh2/

Laurel Pollard
www.laurelpollard.com

The Big Picture

1. What is in the picture? Tell a partner.
2. Tell your teacher the words.
3. Say the words your teacher writes on the board.
4. Write the words on your picture.
5. Look at your partner's book. Are the words in the right places?

Reading

Eduardo Saves a Home

Teaching suggestions on page 137.

1. Eduardo lives in Brazil.

2. He works for a building company.

3. The company tears down old houses.

4. The company builds new houses.

5. Teresa is poor. She lives in an old house.

6. "This house is old," the company says.

7. "We must tear it down!"

8. Eduardo goes to tear down Teresa's house.

9. Teresa cries, "Please don't tear my house down!"

10. Eduardo is poor, too.

11. He goes away.

12. He loses his job.

13. The mayor reads about Eduardo and Teresa in the newspaper.

14. The mayor gives Teresa money.

15. Teresa keeps her house.

16. Eduardo gets another job.

Write the Words You Hear

Your teacher will choose six words or phrases from the story.
Listen to your teacher say the words.
Repeat the word.
Write the word.

1. _____

2. _____

3. _____

4. _____

5. _____

6. _____

Reading without Pictures

Teaching suggestions on page 137.

Eduardo Saves a Home

Eduardo lives in Brazil.
He works for a building company.
The company tears down old houses.
The company builds new houses.
Teresa is poor. She lives in an old house.
"This house is old," the company says.
"We must tear it down!"
Eduardo goes to tear down Teresa's house.
Teresa cries, "Please don't tear my house down!"
Eduardo is poor, too.
He goes away.
He loses his job.
The mayor reads about Eduardo and Teresa in the newspaper.
The mayor gives Teresa money.
Teresa keeps her house.
Eduardo gets another job.

Understanding the Story

Find the Answer

1. Where does Eduardo live? in _____

2. Where does Eduardo work? for a _____

3. What does Eduardo lose? his _____

4. What does the mayor give Teresa? _____

5. What does Teresa keep? her _____

Questions and Answers

Listen to your teacher.
Then take turns reading the questions and answers.

1. Is Teresa poor?   Yes, she is.

2. Is Eduardo rich?   No, he isn't.

3. Is Teresa's house new?   No, it isn't.

4. Is Eduardo's house old?   Yes, it is.

5. Is Eduardo a good man?   Yes, he is.

Circle Yes or No

1. Eduardo works for a building company.	Yes	No
2. The company builds new houses.	Yes	No
3. The company builds old houses.	Yes	No
4. The company tears down new houses.	Yes	No
5. The company tears down old houses.	Yes	No
6. Eduardo goes to Teresa's house.	Yes	No
7. Teresa cries, "Please don't tear my house down!"	Yes	No
8. Eduardo tears down Teresa's house.	Yes	No
9. The mayor gives Eduardo money.	Yes	No
10. Teresa keeps her house.	Yes	No

What Happened First?

What happened first? Write 1 on the line.
What happened second? Write 2 on the line.

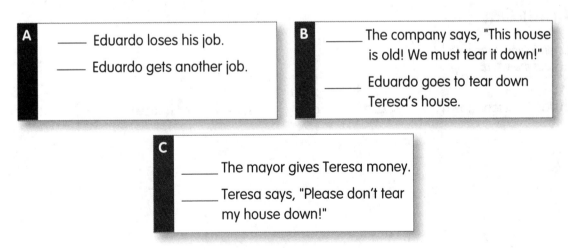

A
_____ Eduardo loses his job.
_____ Eduardo gets another job.

B
_____ The company says, "This house is old! We must tear it down!"
_____ Eduardo goes to tear down Teresa's house.

C
_____ The mayor gives Teresa money.
_____ Teresa says, "Please don't tear my house down!"

Working with Words

Listen, Repeat, and Write

Listen to your teacher say the words.
Repeat each word.
Spell each word.
Write the missing letters.
Then write the words.

lives	works	old	house	down
please	my	job	gives	money

1. l __ __ e s _____

2. __ o r __ s _____

3. __ l d _____

4. __ o u s e _____

5. __ o w __ _____

6. __ __ e a s e _____

7. m __ _____

8. __ o b _____

9. g i __ e s _____

10. __ o __ e y _____

Act It Out

Listen to your teacher.
Act out the word.

build   tear down   please   give   money   house

Matching Sentences with Pictures

What is in the picture?
Write the sentences beside the pictures.

The mayor reads about Eduardo and Teresa in the newspaper.

Teresa keeps her house.

Eduardo works for a building company.

Teresa cries, "Please don't tear my house down!"

"This house is old," the company says.

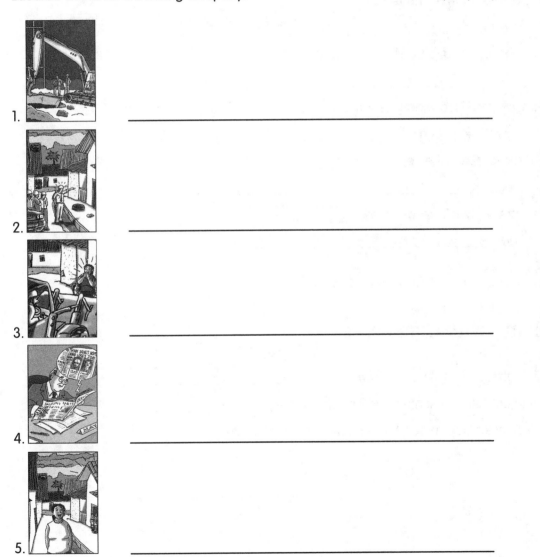

1. _____

2. _____

3. _____

4. _____

5. _____

About Me

Writing About Myself

Listen to your teacher read the sentences.
Repeat the sentences.
Write about yourself in the blanks.

1. Teresa lives in an old house.

    I live in _____.

2. Eduardo works for a building company.

    I _____.

3. Teresa says, "Please don't tear my house down!"

    I say, "Please don't _____."

4. The mayor reads the newspaper.

    I read _____.

5. The mayor gives Teresa money.

    I give _____.

Read the sentences and your answers to a partner.

Talking with Classmates

1. Write about yourself here: **I read** _____.

2. Stand up. Tell your sentence to one classmate.

3. Talk to other classmates. Say the same thing, and listen to them.

Eduardo lives in Brazil.

He works for a building _____.

The company tears down old houses.

The company builds _____ houses.

Teresa is poor. She lives in an old _____.

"This house is old," the company says.

"We must _____ it down!"

Eduardo goes to tear down Teresa's house.

_____ cries, "Please don't tear my house down!"

Eduardo is _____, too.

He goes away.

He loses his _____.

The mayor reads about Eduardo and Teresa

in the _____.

The mayor gives Teresa money.

Teresa _____ her house.

Eduardo gets another job.

Look at the story on page 13.
Make corrections.
Then do Story 1B.

Fill in the Blanks

Eduardo lives in Brazil.

He works for a building _____.

The company tears down old houses.

The company builds _____ houses.

Teresa is poor. She lives in an old _____.

"This house is old," the company says.

"We must _____ it down!"

Eduardo goes to tear down Teresa's house.

_____ cries, "Please don't tear my house down!"

Eduardo is _____, too.

He goes away.

He loses his _____.

The mayor reads about Eduardo and Teresa

in the _____.

The mayor gives Teresa money.

Teresa _____ her house.

Eduardo gets another job.

Look at the story on page 13.
Make corrections.
Then do Story 2A.

Eduardo lives in Brazil.

He _____ for a building company.

The company tears _____ old houses.

The company builds _____ houses.

Teresa is poor. She lives _____ an old house.

"_____ house is old," the company says.

"We must tear _____ down!"

Eduardo goes to _____ down Teresa's house.

Teresa cries, "_____ don't tear my house down!"

Eduardo _____ poor, too.

He goes away.

He _____ his job.

The mayor reads _____ Eduardo and Teresa

in the newspaper.

_____ mayor gives Teresa money.

Teresa keeps her _____.

Eduardo gets another job.

Look at the story on page 13.
Make corrections.
Then do Story 2B.

Fill in the Blanks

Eduardo lives in Brazil.

He _____ for a building company.

The company tears _____ old houses.

The company builds _____ houses.

Teresa is poor. She lives _____ an old house.

"_____ house is old," the company says.

"We must tear _____ down!"

Eduardo goes to _____ down Teresa's house.

Teresa cries, "_____ don't tear my house down!"

Eduardo _____ poor, too.

He goes away.

He _____ his job.

The mayor reads _____ Eduardo and Teresa

in the newspaper.

_____ mayor gives Teresa money.

Teresa keeps her _____.

Eduardo gets another job.

Look at the story on page 13.
Make corrections.
Then do Story 3A.

Eduardo _____ in Brazil.

He _____ _____ a building _____.

The company tears down _____ _____.

The _____ _____ new houses.

Teresa is _____. She _____

_____ an old house.

"This house is old," the company _____.

"We must _____ _____ _____!"

Eduardo _____ to tear down Teresa's _____.

Teresa cries, "_____ _____ tear my

house down!"

Eduardo is poor, too.

_____ goes away.

He loses _____ _____.

The mayor _____ _____ Eduardo

and Teresa in the _____.

The mayor _____ Teresa _____.

Teresa _____ her house.

Eduardo gets another _____.

Look at the story on page 13.
Make corrections.
Then do Story 3B.

Fill in the Blanks

Eduardo _____ in Brazil.

He _____ _____ a building _____.

The company tears down _____ _____.

The _____ _____ new houses.

Teresa is _____. She _____

_____ an old house.

"This house is old," the company _____.

"We must _____ _____ _____!"

Eduardo _____ to tear down Teresa's _____.

Teresa cries, "_____ _____ tear my

house down!"

Eduardo is poor, too.

_____ goes away.

He loses _____ _____.

The mayor _____ _____ Eduardo

and Teresa in the _____.

The mayor _____ Teresa _____.

Teresa _____ her house.

Eduardo gets another _____.

Look at the story on page 13.
Make corrections.

The Big Picture

1. What is in the picture? Tell a partner.
2. Tell your teacher the words.
3. Say the words your teacher writes on the board.
4. Write the words on your picture.
5. Look at your partner's book. Are the words in the right places?

Reading

The 75-Year Friendship

Teaching suggestions on page 137.

1929 January 1929						
S	M	T	W	T	F	S
				1	2	3
4	5	6	7	8	9	10
11	12	13	14	15	16	17
18	19	20	21	22	23	24
25	26	27	28	29	30	31

1. It is 1929.

2. Darwin and Art are 12 years old.

3. They are best friends.

4. They go hunting together.

5. A wildcat attacks Darwin.

6. Darwin cries and is afraid.

7. Art shoots the wildcat.

8. He saves Darwin's life.

9. It is now 2004.

10. Darwin and Art live in San Francisco.

11. They are 87 years old.

12. Both men are widowers.

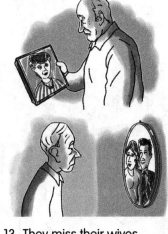

13. They miss their wives.

14. They talk together about many things.

15. It is good to have a best friend.

Write the Words You Hear

Your teacher will choose six words or phrases from the story.
Listen to your teacher.
Repeat the word.
Write the word.

1. _____

2. _____

3. _____

4. _____

5. _____

6. _____

Reading without Pictures

Teaching suggestions on page 137.

The 75-Year Friendship

It is 1929.
Darwin and Art are 12 years old.
They are best friends.
They go hunting together.
A wildcat attacks Darwin.
Darwin cries and is afraid.
Art shoots the wildcat.
He saves Darwin's life.
It is now 2004.
Darwin and Art live in San Francisco.
They are 87 years old.
Both men are widowers.
They miss their wives.
They talk together about many things.
It is good to have a best friend.

Understanding the Story

Find the Answer

1. What attacks Darwin? a _____

2. Who shoots the wildcat? _____

3. Where does Art live in 2004? _____

4. Where does Darwin live in 2004? _____

5. Who do Darwin and Art miss? their _____

Questions and Answers

Listen to your teacher.
Then take turns reading the questions and answers.

1. In 1929, are Darwin and Art 14 years old?   No, they aren't.

2. Are they best friends?   Yes, they are.

3. In 1929, is Darwin afraid?   Yes, he is.

4. Is Darwin alive in 1929?   Yes, he is.

5. In 2004, are Darwin and Art 45 years old?   No, they aren't.

6. In 2004, are Darwin and Art in San Francisco?   Yes, they are.

7. In 1929, are Darwin and Art widowers?   No, they aren't.

8. Is it good to have a best friend?   Yes, it is.

Circle Yes or No

1. Darwin and Art are 12 years old in 1929.   Yes   No
2. Darwin and Art are best friends.   Yes   No
3. A wild dog attacks Darwin.   Yes   No
4. Darwin shoots the wildcat.   Yes   No
5. Art shoots the wildcat.   Yes   No
6. In 2004, Darwin and Art live in Chicago.   Yes   No
7. In 2004, Darwin and Art are 50 years old.   Yes   No
8. In 2004, Darwin and Art are widowers.   Yes   No
9. Darwin and Art miss their wives.   Yes   No
10. It is good to have a best friend.   Yes   No

What Happened First?

What happened first? Write 1 on the line.
What happened second? Write 2 on the line.

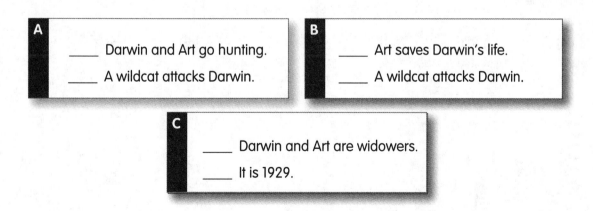

A

_____ Darwin and Art go hunting.

_____ A wildcat attacks Darwin.

B

_____ Art saves Darwin's life.

_____ A wildcat attacks Darwin.

C

_____ Darwin and Art are widowers.

_____ It is 1929.

Working with Words

Categories

Write the words in the right places.

twelve   friends   nineteen-twenty-nine   Darwin

two thousand and four   wives   wildcat   eighty-seven

widowers   Art

Numbers	People	Animals
twelve	friends	

Act It Out

Listen to your teacher.
Act out the word.

hunt   afraid   talk   shoot   wildcat   cry

Matching Sentences with Pictures

What is in the picture?
Write the sentences beside the pictures.

It is good to have a best friend.   Art saves Darwin's life.

They miss their wives.   Darwin and Art go hunting together.

A wildcat attacks Darwin.

1. _____

2. _____

3. _____

4. _____

5. _____

About Me

Writing About Myself

Listen to your teacher read the sentences.
Repeat the sentences.
Write about yourself in the blanks.

1. Darwin and Art are 12 years old.

    I am _____ years old.

2. They go hunting together.

    My friend and I _____ together.

3. Darwin and Art live in San Francisco.

    I live in _____.

4. Darwin and Art miss their wives.

    I miss _____.

5. It is good to have a best friend.

    It is good to have _____.

Read the sentences and your answers to a partner.

Talking with Classmates

1. Write about yourself here: **My friend** _____.

2. Stand up. Tell your sentence to one classmate.

3. Talk to other classmates. Say the same thing, and listen to them.

_____ is 1929.

Darwin and Art are 12 years old.

_____ are best friends.

They go hunting together.

A _____ attacks Darwin.

Darwin cries and is afraid.

Art shoots _____ wildcat.

He saves Darwin's life.

It is now 2004.

_____ and Art live in San Francisco.

They are 87 years _____.

Both men are widowers.

They miss their wives.

They _____ together about many things.

It is good to have a _____ friend.

Look at the story on page 29.
Make corrections.
Then do Story 1B.

_____ is 1929.

Darwin and Art are 12 years old.

_____ are best friends.

They go hunting together.

A _____ attacks Darwin.

Darwin cries and is afraid.

Art shoots _____ wildcat.

He saves Darwin's life.

It is now 2004.

_____ and Art live in San Francisco.

They are 87 years _____.

Both men are widowers.

They miss their wives.

They _____ together about many things.

It is good to have a _____ friend.

Look at the story on page 29.
Make corrections.
Then do Story 2A.

It _____ 1929.

Darwin and Art are 12 _____ old.

They are best friends.

They _____ hunting together.

A wildcat attacks Darwin.

Darwin _____ and is afraid.

Art shoots _____ wildcat.

He saves Darwin's life.

It is _____ 2004.

Darwin and Art live _____ San Francisco.

They are 87 years old.

Both _____ are widowers.

They miss their wives.

_____ talk together about many things.

It _____ good to have a best _____.

Look at the story on page 29.
Make corrections.
Then do Story 2B.

Fill in the Blanks

It _____ 1929.

Darwin and Art are 12 _____ old.

They are best friends.

They _____ hunting together.

A wildcat attacks Darwin.

Darwin _____ and is afraid.

Art shoots _____ wildcat.

He saves Darwin's life.

It is _____ 2004.

Darwin and Art live _____ San Francisco.

They are 87 years old.

Both _____ are widowers.

They miss their wives.

_____ talk together about many things.

It _____ good to have a best _____.

Look at the story on page 29.
Make corrections.
Then do Story 3A.

It is 1929.

Darwin _____ Art _____

12 years _____.

They are best _____.

They go hunting together.

_____ wildcat attacks Darwin.

_____ cries and is _____.

Art _____ the wildcat.

He saves Darwin's _____.

It is _____ 2004.

Darwin and Art _____

_____ San Francisco.

_____ _____ 87 years old.

Both men _____ widowers.

They miss their _____.

They talk together _____ many _____.

It is good _____ _____ a best friend.

Look at the story on page 29.
Make corrections.
Then do Story 3B.

It is 1929.

Darwin _____ Art _____

12 years _____.

They are best _____.

They go hunting together.

_____ wildcat attacks Darwin.

_____ cries and is _____.

Art _____ the wildcat.

He saves Darwin's _____.

It is _____ 2004.

Darwin and Art _____

_____ San Francisco.

_____ _____ 87 years old.

Both men _____ widowers.

They miss their _____.

They talk together _____ many _____.

It is good _____ _____ a best friend.

Look at the story on page 29.
Make corrections.

The Big Picture

1. What is in the picture? Tell a partner.
2. Tell your teacher the words.
3. Say the words your teacher writes on the board.
4. Write the words on your picture.
5. Look at your partner's book. Are the words in the right places?

Reading

Maria Finds a Friend

Teaching suggestions on page 137.

1. Maria is a new student at Watsbury High School.

2. She has no friends.

3. She looks at all the girls.

4. They have pretty clothes.

5. They have friends.

6. Nobody talks to Maria.

7. One day, Lucia smiles and talks to Maria.

8. Maria is happy. She thinks, "I have a friend!"

9. Lucia takes Maria to a party.

10. Everybody smokes and drinks beer.

11. Maria doesn't like this party.

12. She is alone again.

13. Maria meets Eva in the library.

14. The girls study together.

15. They go shopping together.

16. They go to movies together.

17. Eva is a good friend for Maria!

Write the Words You Hear

Your teacher will choose six words or phrases from the story.
Listen to your teacher.
Repeat the word.
Write the word.

1. _____   4. _____

2. _____   5. _____

3. _____   6. _____

Reading without Pictures

Teaching suggestions on page 137.

Maria Finds a Friend

Maria is a new student at Watsbury High School.
She has no friends.
She looks at all the girls.
They have pretty clothes.
They have friends.
Nobody talks to Maria.
One day, Lucia smiles and talks to Maria.
Maria is happy. She thinks, "I have a friend!"
Lucia takes Maria to a party.
Everybody smokes and drinks beer.
Maria doesn't like this party.
She is alone again.
Maria meets Eva in the library.
The girls study together.
They go shopping together.
They go to movies together.
Eva is a good friend for Maria!

Understanding the Story

Find the Answer

1. Who talks to Maria in school? _____

2. Who takes Maria to a party? _____

3. Who smokes and drinks beer at the party? _____

5. Where does Maria meet Eva? in the _____

Questions and Answers

Listen to your teacher.
Then take turns reading the questions and answers.

1. Is Maria a new student at Watsbury High School?   Yes, she is.

2. Is Maria a high school student?   Yes, she is.

3. Is Maria lonely?   Yes, she is.

4. Lucia speaks to Maria. Is Maria happy?   Yes, she is.

5. Is Maria happy at the party?   No, she isn't.

6. Is Lucia a good friend for Maria?   No, she isn't.

7. After the party, is Maria alone again?   Yes, she is.

8. Is Eva a good friend for Maria?   Yes, she is.

Circle Yes or No

1. Maria has many friends.   Yes   No
2. The girls in high school have pretty clothes.   Yes   No
3. The girls in high school have friends.   Yes   No
4. At first, nobody talks to Maria.   Yes   No
5. One day Lucia smiles and talks to Maria.   Yes   No
6. Lucia takes Maria to a party.   Yes   No
7. Maria likes the party.   Yes   No
8. Maria meets Eva at the party.   Yes   No
9. Maria and Eva go to movies together.   Yes   No
10. Maria and Eva smoke and drink beer.   Yes   No

What Happened First?

What happened first? Write 1 on the line.
What happened second? Write 2 on the line.

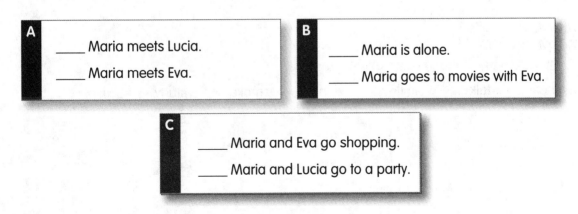

A
_____ Maria meets Lucia.
_____ Maria meets Eva.

B
_____ Maria is alone.
_____ Maria goes to movies with Eva.

C
_____ Maria and Eva go shopping.
_____ Maria and Lucia go to a party.

Working with Words

Listen, Repeat, and Write

Listen to your teacher say the words.
Repeat each word.
Spell each word.
Write the missing letters.
Then write the words.

girls   friend   smiles   clothes   study

party   alone   shopping   movies   happy

1. f r i __ __ d   _____   6. p a __ __ y   _____

2. g i __ __ s   _____   7. a l __ n e   _____

3. c l __ t h __ s   _____   8. s t __ __ y   _____

4. s m i __ __ s   _____   9. s h o __ __ __ __ g   _____

5. h a __ __ y   _____   10. m o __ __ __ s   _____

Act It Out

Listen to your teacher.
Act out the word.

clothes   talk   smile   drink   smoke   study   think

Matching Sentences with Pictures

What is in the picture?
Write the sentences beside the pictures.

Maria meets Eva in the library.

Eva is a good friend for Maria!

One day, Lucia smiles and talks to Maria.

Maria doesn't like this party.

Maria has no friends.

1. _____

2. _____

3. _____

4. _____

5. _____

About Me

Writing About Myself

Listen to your teacher read the sentences.
Repeat the sentences.
Write about yourself in the blanks.

1. Maria is a student.

   I am _____.

2. Maria has a friend.

   I have _____.

3. Lucia drinks beer.

   I drink _____.

4. Maria and Eva study in the library.

   I study _____.

5. They go shopping.

   I _____.

Read the sentences and your answers to a partner.

Talking with Classmates

1. Write about yourself here: **I go** _____.

2. Stand up. Tell your sentence to one classmate.

3. Talk to other classmates. Say the same thing, and listen to them.

Maria is a new _____ at Watsbury High School.

She has no friends.

She _____ at all the girls.

They have pretty clothes.

_____ have friends.

Nobody talks to Maria.

One day, Lucia _____ and talks to Maria.

Maria is happy. She thinks, "_____ have a friend!"

Lucia takes Maria to a _____.

Everybody smokes and drinks beer.

Maria doesn't _____ this party.

She is alone again.

Maria meets Eva _____ the library.

The girls study together.

They go shopping _____.

They go to movies together.

Eva is a good _____ for Maria!

Look at the story on page 45.
Make corrections.
Then do Story 1B.

Fill in the Blanks

Maria is a new _____ at Watsbury High School.

She has no friends.

She _____ at all the girls.

They have pretty clothes.

_____ have friends.

Nobody talks to Maria.

One day, Lucia _____ and talks to Maria.

Maria is happy. She thinks, "_____ have a friend!"

Lucia takes Maria to a _____.

Everybody smokes and drinks beer.

Maria doesn't _____ this party.

She is alone again.

Maria meets Eva _____ the library.

The girls study together.

They go shopping _____.

They go to movies together.

Eva is a good _____ for Maria!

Look at the story on page 45.
Make corrections.
Then do Story 2A.

Maria is a _____ student at Watsbury High School.

She _____ no friends.

She looks at all the _____.

They have pretty clothes.

They have _____.

Nobody talks to Maria.

One day, Lucia smiles _____ talks to Maria.

Maria is happy. _____ thinks, "I have a friend!"

Lucia _____ Maria to a party.

Everybody smokes and drinks _____.

Maria doesn't like this party.

She is _____ again.

Maria meets Eva in the _____.

The girls study together.

They go _____ together.

They go to movies together.

Eva _____ a good friend for Maria!

Look at the story on page 45.
Make corrections.
Then do Story 2B.

Maria is a _____ student at Watsbury High School.

She _____ no friends.

She looks at all the _____.

They have pretty clothes.

They have _____.

Nobody talks to Maria.

One day, Lucia smiles _____ talks to Maria.

Maria is happy. _____ thinks, "I have a friend!"

Lucia _____ Maria to a party.

Everybody smokes and drinks _____.

Maria doesn't like this party.

She is _____ again.

Maria meets Eva in the _____.

The girls study together.

They go _____ together.

They go to movies together.

Eva _____ a good friend for Maria!

Look at the story on page 45.
Make corrections.
Then do Story 3A.

Fill in the Blanks

Maria _____ a new _____

at Watsbury High _____.

She has _____ friends.

She looks _____ all the girls.

They _____ pretty clothes.

They have _____.

Nobody talks _____ Maria.

One _____, Lucia smiles _____

_____ to Maria.

Maria is _____. She thinks, "I have

_____ friend!"

Lucia takes Maria _____ a party.

Everybody _____ _____ drinks beer.

Maria doesn't _____ this _____.

She is alone _____.

Maria meets Eva _____ the _____.

The girls study _____.

They _____ _____ together.

They go to _____ together.

Eva is a _____ friend for Maria!

Look at the story on page 45.
Make corrections.
Then do Story 3B.

Maria _____ a new _____

at Watsbury High _____.

She has _____ friends.

She looks _____ all the girls.

They _____ pretty clothes.

They have _____.

Nobody talks _____ Maria.

One _____, Lucia smiles _____

_____ to Maria.

Maria is _____. She thinks, "I have

_____ friend!"

Lucia takes Maria _____ a party.

Everybody _____ _____ drinks beer.

Maria doesn't _____ this _____.

She is alone _____.

Maria meets Eva _____ the _____.

The girls study _____.

They _____ _____ together.

They go to _____ together.

Eva is a _____ friend for Maria!

Look at the story on page 45.
Make corrections.

The Big Picture

1. What is in the picture? Tell a partner.
2. Tell your teacher the words.
3. Say the words your teacher writes on the board.
4. Write the words on your picture.
5. Look at your partner's book. Are the words in the right places?

Reading

Lost and Found

Teaching suggestions on page 137.

1. It is 1963, and Gulli is 18 years old. 2. She lives in Sweden. 3. In her wallet are pictures of her family and her boyfriend.

  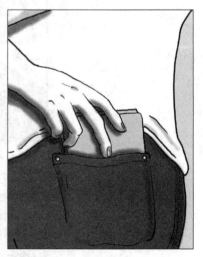

4. In her wallet she has 90 kronor. 5. 90 kronor is Gulli's rent. 6. Gulli puts her wallet in her pocket.

7. She rides her bicycle to work.

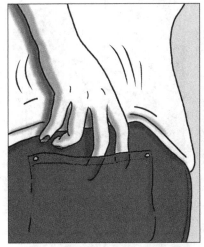
8. Gulli puts her hand in her pocket.

9. Her wallet is not there.

10. Her wallet is lost!

11. It is 2003, and Gulli is 58 years old.

12. A package comes.

13. Her wallet is in the package.

14. The pictures and the money are there.

15. A note is in the package.

16. The note says, "Surprise!"

Write the Words You Hear

Your teacher will choose six words or phrases from the story.
Listen to your teacher.
Repeat the word.
Write the word.

1. _____

2. _____

3. _____

4. _____

5. _____

6. _____

Reading without Pictures

Teaching suggestions on page 137.

Lost and Found

It is 1963, and Gulli is 18 years old.
She lives in Sweden.
In her wallet are pictures of her family and her boyfriend.
In her wallet she has 90 kronor.
90 kronor is Gulli's rent.
Gulli puts her wallet in her pocket.
She rides her bicycle to work.
Gulli puts her hand in her pocket.
Her wallet is not there.
Her wallet is lost!
It is 2003, and Gulli is 58 years old.
A package comes.
Her wallet is in the package.
The pictures and the money are there.
A note is in the package.
The note says, "Surprise!"

Understanding the Story

Find the Answer

1. Where does Gulli live? in _____

2. What is in Gulli's wallet? _____

3. Where does Gulli put her hand? in her _____

4. Where is the note? in the _____

5. What does the note say? _____

Questions and Answers

Listen to your teacher.
Then take turns reading the questions and answers.

1. In 1963, is Gulli 50 years old?   No, she isn't.

2. Is Gulli's rent 100 kronor?   No, it isn't.

3. Is the wallet in Gulli's pocket?   No, it isn't.

4. Is the wallet lost?   Yes, it is.

5. In 2003, is Gulli 88 years old?   No, she isn't.

6. Is Gulli's wallet in the package?   Yes, it is.

7. Are the pictures and the money still in the wallet?   Yes, they are.

8. Is a note in the package?   Yes, it is.

Circle Yes or No

1. Gulli is 18 years old in 1963. Yes No
2. Gulli lives in Australia. Yes No
3. Gulli rides her bicycle to work. Yes No
4. Gulli's rent is 120 kronor. Yes No
5. Gulli's wallet is lost. Yes No
6. In 2003, a package comes. Yes No
7. A book is in the package. Yes No
8. Gulli's wallet is in the package. Yes No
9. The pictures and money are still in the wallet. Yes No
10. A note is in the package. Yes No

What Happened First?

What happened first? Write 1 on the line.
What happened second? Write 2 on the line.

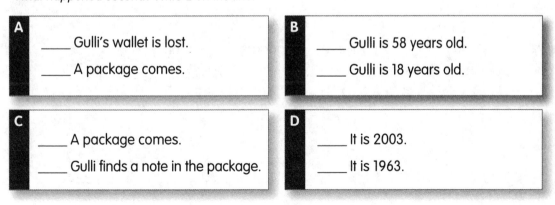

A

_____ Gulli's wallet is lost.

_____ A package comes.

B

_____ Gulli is 58 years old.

_____ Gulli is 18 years old.

C

_____ A package comes.

_____ Gulli finds a note in the package.

D

_____ It is 2003.

_____ It is 1963.

Working with Words

Put the Words in the Spaces

note   wallet   rent   bicycle

picture   package   pocket

1. Gulli puts money and pictures in her _____.

2. Gulli rides her _____ to work.

3. There is a _____ of Gulli's family in her wallet.

4. Gulli's _____ is 90 kronor.

5. Gulli puts her wallet in her _____.

6. In 2003, a _____ comes to Gulli.

7. Her wallet and a _____ are in the package.

Act It Out

Listen to your teacher.
Act out the word.

bicycle   hand   pocket   package   money

Matching Sentences with Pictures

What is in the picture?
Write the sentences beside the pictures.

Gulli puts her wallet in her pocket.   Gulli's wallet is in the package.

Her wallet is lost!   It is 2003, and Gulli is 58 years old.

She rides her bicycle to work.

1. _____

2. _____

3. _____

4. _____

5. _____

About Me

Writing About Myself

Listen to your teacher read the sentences.
Repeat the sentences.
Write about yourself in the blanks.

1. It is 1963, and Gulli is 18 years old.

    It is _____, and I am _____ years old.

2. Gulli rides a bicycle.

    I _____.

3. Gulli has a wallet.

    I have _____.

4. Gulli has a picture of her boyfriend.

    I have a picture of _____.

5. Gulli lost her wallet.

    I lost _____.

Read the sentences and your answers to a partner.

Talking with Classmates

1. Write about yourself here:

    I have _____ **in my wallet/my purse/my pocket.**

2. Stand up. Tell your sentence to one classmate.

3. Talk to other classmates. Say the same thing, and listen to them.

It _____ 1963, and Gulli is 18 years old.

She lives _____ Sweden.

In her wallet are pictures of her family

and _____ boyfriend.

In her wallet she has 90 kronor.

_____ kronor is Gulli's rent.

Gulli puts her wallet in her _____.

She rides her bicycle to work.

Gulli puts her _____ in her pocket.

Her wallet is not there.

Her _____ is lost!

It is 2003, and Gulli is 58 _____ old.

A package comes.

Her wallet is in the _____.

The pictures and the money are there.

A _____ is in the package.

The note says, "Surprise!"

Look at the story on page 61.
Make corrections.
Then do Story 1B.

It _____ 1963, and Gulli is 18 years old.

She lives _____ Sweden.

In her wallet are pictures of her family

and _____ boyfriend.

In her wallet she has 90 kronor.

_____ kronor is Gulli's rent.

Gulli puts her wallet in her _____.

She rides her bicycle to work.

Gulli puts her _____ in her pocket.

Her wallet is not there.

Her _____ is lost!

It is 2003, and Gulli is 58 _____ old.

A package comes.

Her wallet is in the _____.

The pictures and the money are there.

A _____ is in the package.

The note says, "Surprise!"

Look at the story on page 61.
Make corrections.
Then do Story 2A.

_____ is 1963, and Gulli is

18 _____ old.

She lives in Sweden.

_____ her wallet are pictures of her

_____ and her boyfriend.

In her _____ she has 90 kronor.

90 kronor _____ Gulli's rent.

Gulli puts her wallet _____ her pocket.

She rides her bicycle _____ work.

Gulli puts her hand _____ her pocket.

Her wallet is not _____.

Her wallet is lost!

It _____ 2003, and Gulli is

58 years _____.

A package comes.

_____ wallet is in the package.

_____ pictures and the money are _____.

A note is in the _____.

The note _____, "Surprise!"

Look at the story on page 61.
Make corrections.
Then do Story 2B.

_____ is 1963, and Gulli is

18 _____ old.

She lives in Sweden.

_____ her wallet are pictures of her

_____ and her boyfriend.

In her _____ she has 90 kronor.

90 kronor _____ Gulli's rent.

Gulli puts her wallet _____ her pocket.

She rides her bicycle _____ work.

Gulli puts her hand _____ her pocket.

Her wallet is not _____.

Her wallet is lost!

It _____ 2003, and Gulli is

58 years _____.

A package comes.

_____ wallet is in the package.

_____ pictures and the money are _____.

A note is in the _____.

The note _____, "Surprise!"

Look at the story on page 61.
Make corrections.
Then do Story 3A.

It is 1963, _____ Gulli is

18 _____ _____.

She _____ in Sweden.

In her wallet are _____ of _____

_____ and her boyfriend.

In her wallet _____ _____ 90 kronor.

90 kronor _____ Gulli's rent.

Gulli puts _____ _____ in her pocket.

She _____ her bicycle to _____.

Gulli puts _____ _____ in her pocket.

Her wallet is _____ _____.

Her wallet _____ lost!

_____ _____ 2003, and Gulli is

58 years old.

_____ _____ comes.

Her wallet is _____ the package.

The pictures and _____ _____

are there.

A note is in _____ _____.

The note says, "_____!"

Look at the story on page 61.
Make corrections.
Then do Story 3B.

Fill in the Blanks

It is 1963, _____ Gulli is

18 _____ _____.

She _____ in Sweden.

In her wallet are _____ of _____

_____ and her boyfriend.

In her wallet _____ _____ 90 kronor.

90 kronor _____ Gulli's rent.

Gulli puts _____ _____ in her pocket.

She _____ her bicycle to _____.

Gulli puts _____ _____ in her pocket.

Her wallet is _____ _____.

Her wallet _____ lost!

_____ _____ 2003, and Gulli is

58 years old.

_____ _____ comes.

Her wallet is _____ the package.

The pictures and _____ _____

are there.

A note is in _____ _____.

The note says, "_____!"

Look at the story on page 61.
Make corrections.

The Big Picture

1. What is in the picture? Tell a partner.
2. Tell your teacher the words.
3. Say the words your teacher writes on the board.
4. Write the words on your picture.
5. Look at your partner's book. Are the words in the right places?

Reading

Meeting the New Neighbor

Teaching suggestions on page 137.

1. Elizabeth is from Liberia.

2. She comes to Tucson, Arizona.

3. She lives in Apartment 1C.

4. The apartment has a kitchen, a living room, a bedroom, and a bathroom.

5. Charles is from Liberia, too.

6. He lives in Apartment 3D.

7. He lives alone. He sits on his sofa.

8. He thinks about his mother and his father.

9. He thinks about his brother and his sister. He is sad.

10. A neighbor says to Charles, "A woman from Liberia lives in Apartment 1C."

11. The neighbor asks, "Do you want to meet her?"

12. Charles goes to Elizabeth's apartment.

13. Elizabeth opens the door. She smiles.   14. They laugh.

15. They cry.

16. They hug. Elizabeth is Charles's sister!

Write the Words You Hear

Your teacher will choose six words or phrases from the story.
Listen to your teacher.
Repeat the word.
Write the word.

1. _____   4. _____

2. _____   5. _____

3. _____   6. _____

Reading without Pictures

Teaching suggestions on page 137.

Meeting the New Neighbor

Elizabeth is from Liberia.
She comes to Tucson, Arizona
She lives in Apartment 1C.
The apartment has a kitchen, a living room, a bedroom, and a bathroom.
Charles is from Liberia, too.
He lives in Apartment 3D.
He lives alone. He sits on his sofa.
He thinks about his mother and his father.
He thinks about his brother and his sister. He is sad.
A neighbor says to Charles, "A woman from Liberia lives in Apartment 1C."
The neighbor asks, "Do you want to meet her?"
Charles goes to Elizabeth's apartment.
Elizabeth opens the door. She smiles.
They laugh.
They cry.
They hug. Elizabeth is Charles's sister!

Understanding the Story

Find the Answer

1. Who says, "A woman from Liberia lives in Apartment 1C. Do you want to meet her?"

    a _____

2. Who opens the door? _____

3. Who laughs? _____ and _____

4. Who hugs? _____ and _____

5. Who is Elizabeth? Charles's _____

Questions and Answers

Listen to your teacher.
Then take turns reading the questions and answers.

1. Is Elizabeth from Liberia?   Yes, she is.

2. Charles is from South Africa.   No, he isn't.

3. Is Charles alone in his apartment?   Yes, he is.

4. Is Charles happy in his apartment?   No, he isn't.

5. Is Charles happy to see Elizabeth?   Yes, he is.

6. Is Elizabeth happy to see Charles?   Yes, she is.

7. Is Elizabeth his sister?   Yes, she is.

8. Is Elizabeth his mother?   No, she isn't.

Circle Yes or No

1. Elizabeth is from Tucson, Arizona.	Yes	No
2. Elizabeth lives in Apartment 1C.	Yes	No
3. Elizabeth's apartment has three bedrooms.	Yes	No
4. Charles is from Tucson, too.	Yes	No
5. Charles lives in Apartment 3D.	Yes	No
6. Charles lives with his brother.	Yes	No
7. Charles thinks about his mother and father.	Yes	No
8. A neighbor talks to Charles.	Yes	No
9. Elizabeth goes to Charles's apartment.	Yes	No
10. Elizabeth is Charles's sister!	Yes	No

What Happened First?

What happened first? Write 1 on the line.
What happened second? Write 2 on the line.

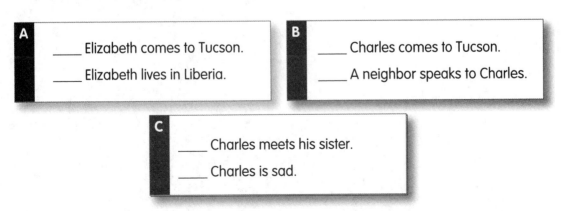

A

_____ Elizabeth comes to Tucson.

_____ Elizabeth lives in Liberia.

B

_____ Charles comes to Tucson.

_____ A neighbor speaks to Charles.

C

_____ Charles meets his sister.

_____ Charles is sad.

Working with Words

Categories

Write the words in the right places.

mother   bathroom   living room   sister

brother   bedroom   kitchen   father

Rooms in an Apartment	People in a Family
bathroom	mother

Act It Out

Listen to your teacher.
Act out the word.

think   sit down   stand up   smile   laugh   cry   hug

Matching Sentences with Pictures

What is in the picture?
Write the sentences beside the pictures.

They hug. Elizabeth is Charles's sister!

Charles thinks about his brother and sister. He is sad.

Charles goes to Elizabeth's apartment.

Charles lives in Apartment 3D.

Elizabeth lives in Apartment 1C.

1. _____

2. _____

3. _____

4. _____

5. _____

About Me

Writing About Myself

Listen to your teacher read the sentences.
Repeat the sentences.
Write about yourself in the blanks.

1. Elizabeth and Charles are from Liberia. I am from _____.

2. Charles lives alone. I live _____.

3. Charles thinks about his mother and his father. I think about _____.

4. Charles is sad. I am _____.

5. Charles talks with his neighbor. I talk with _____.

6. Charles goes to Elizabeth's apartment. I go to _____.

7. Charles laughs with his sister. I laugh with _____.

Circle Yes or No.

8. I am sad today.   Yes   No

9. I have a sister.   Yes   No

10. I have a brother.   Yes   No

Read the sentences and your answers to a partner.

Talking with Classmates

1. Write about yourself here: **I am from** _____.
2. Stand up. Tell your sentence to one classmate.
3. Talk to other classmates. Say the same thing, and listen to them.

4. Write about yourself here: **I think about** _____.
5. Stand up. Tell your sentence to one classmate.
6. Talk to other classmates. Say the same thing, and listen to them.

Elizabeth is from Liberia.

She comes to Tucson, Arizona.

_____ lives in Apartment 1C.

The apartment has a kitchen, _____ living room,

a bedroom, and a bathroom.

Charles is from _____, too.

He lives in Apartment 3D.

He lives alone. _____ sits on his sofa.

He thinks about his mother _____ his father.

He thinks about his brother and his _____.

He is sad.

A neighbor says to Charles, "A _____ from Liberia

lives in Apartment 1C."

The neighbor asks, "Do you want _____ meet her?"

Charles goes to Elizabeth's apartment.

Elizabeth opens _____ door. She smiles.

They laugh.

They cry.

They hug. _____ is Charles's sister!

Look at the story on page 77.
Make corrections.
Then do Story 1B.

Elizabeth is from Liberia.

She comes to Tucson, Arizona.

_____ lives in Apartment 1C.

The apartment has a kitchen, _____ living room,

a bedroom, and a bathroom.

Charles is from _____, too.

He lives in Apartment 3D.

He lives alone. _____ sits on his sofa.

He thinks about his mother _____ his father.

He thinks about his brother and his _____.

He is sad.

A neighbor says to Charles, "A _____ from Liberia

lives in Apartment 1C."

The neighbor asks, "Do you want _____ meet her?"

Charles goes to Elizabeth's apartment.

Elizabeth opens _____ door. She smiles.

They laugh.

They cry.

They hug. _____ is Charles's sister!

Look at the story on page 77.
Make corrections.
Then do Story 2A.

Elizabeth is _____ Liberia.

She comes _____ Tucson, Arizona

She lives _____ Apartment 1C.

The _____ has a kitchen, a _____ room, a bedroom, and _____ bathroom.

Charles _____ from Liberia, too.

He lives _____ Apartment 3D.

He lives _____. He sits on his _____.

He thinks about his _____ and his father.

He _____ about his brother and _____ sister. He is _____.

A neighbor _____ to Charles, "A woman from Liberia _____ in Apartment 1C."

The neighbor _____, "Do _____ want to meet her?"

Charles _____ to Elizabeth's apartment.

Elizabeth _____ the door. She smiles.

_____ laugh.

They _____.

They hug. Elizabeth _____ Charles's sister!

Look at the story on page 77.
Make corrections.
Then do Story 2B.

Fill in the Blanks

Elizabeth is _____ Liberia.

She comes _____ Tucson, Arizona

She lives _____ Apartment 1C.

The _____ has a kitchen, a _____

room, a bedroom, and _____ bathroom.

Charles _____ from Liberia, too.

He lives _____ Apartment 3D.

He lives _____. He sits on his _____.

He thinks about his _____ and his father.

He _____ about his brother and

_____ sister. He is _____.

A neighbor _____ to Charles, "A woman from Liberia

_____ in Apartment 1C."

The neighbor _____, "Do _____

want to meet her?"

Charles _____ to Elizabeth's apartment.

Elizabeth _____ the door. She smiles.

_____ laugh.

They _____.

They hug. Elizabeth _____ Charles's sister!

Look at the story on page 77.
Make corrections.
Then do Story 3A.

Elizabeth _____ _____ Liberia.

She comes _____ Tucson, Arizona.

She _____ _____ Apartment 1C.

The _____ _____ a kitchen, a living

_____, a bedroom, and a _____.

Charles is _____ Liberia, too.

_____ _____ in Apartment 3D.

He lives alone. He _____ on his sofa.

He _____ _____ his mother and

_____ _____.

He _____ about his brother _____

_____ sister. He _____ sad.

A neighbor says to _____, "A _____

from Liberia lives in _____ 1C."

The neighbor asks, "Do _____ _____

to meet her?"

Charles goes _____ Elizabeth's _____.

Elizabeth _____ the _____. She smiles.

They _____.

_____ cry.

They hug. _____ is Charles's _____!

Look at the story on page 77.
Make corrections.
Then do Story 3B.

Elizabeth _____ _____ Liberia.

She comes _____ Tucson, Arizona.

She _____ _____ Apartment 1C.

The _____ _____ a kitchen, a living

_____, a bedroom, and a _____.

Charles is _____ Liberia, too.

_____ _____ in Apartment 3D.

He lives alone. He _____ on his sofa.

He _____ _____ his mother and

_____ _____.

He _____ about his brother _____

_____ sister. He _____ sad.

A neighbor says to _____, "A _____

from Liberia lives in _____ 1C."

The neighbor asks, "Do _____ _____

to meet her?"

Charles goes _____ Elizabeth's _____.

Elizabeth _____ the _____. She smiles.

They _____.

_____ cry.

They hug. _____ is Charles's _____!

Look at the story on page 77.
Make corrections.

The Big Picture

1. What is in the picture? Tell a partner.
2. Tell your teacher the words.
3. Say the words your teacher writes on the board.
4. Write the words on your picture.
5. Look at your partner's book. Are the words in the right places?

Reading

The Translator

Teaching suggestions on page 137.

1. Lucas Silva lives in Georgia.

2. He is twelve years old.

3. He is from Brazil.

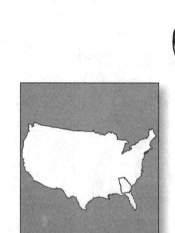

¡Hola! Oi! Hello!

¡Hola! Oi!

4. He speaks Spanish, Portuguese, and English.

5. His family and friends speak Spanish or Portuguese.

6. But they don't speak English.

7. Lucas's father has a carpet business.

8. Lucas makes phone calls for his father.

9. A boy cuts his knee.

10. Lucas fills in forms at the hospital.

11. He translates for the family.

12. Lucas's sister wants a job.

13. He translates job ads for her.

14. His sister finds a job.

15. Lucas helps a woman buy a car.

16. He helps new kids at school.

17. Lucas misses Brazil.

18. But he likes the United States.

19. For Lucas, helping people is fun!

Write the Words You Hear

Your teacher will choose six words or phrases from the story.
Listen to your teacher.
Repeat the word.
Write the word.

1. _____

2. _____

3. _____

4. _____

5. _____

6. _____

Reading without Pictures

Teaching suggestions on page 137.

The Translator

Lucas Silva lives in Georgia.
He is twelve years old.
He is from Brazil.
He speaks Spanish, Portuguese, and English.
His family and friends speak Spanish or Portuguese.
But they don't speak English.
Lucas's father has a carpet business.
Lucas makes phone calls for his father.
A boy cuts his knee.
Lucas fills in forms at the hospital.
He translates for the family.
Lucas's sister wants a job.
He translates job ads for her.
His sister finds a job.
Lucas helps a woman buy a car.
He helps new kids at school.
Lucas misses Brazil.
But he likes the United States.
For Lucas, helping people is fun!

Understanding the Story

Find the Answer

1. Where does Lucas fill in forms? at the _____

2. What does Lucas's sister want? a _____

3. What does Lucas help a woman to buy? a _____

4. What does Lucas miss? _____

5. What does Lucas like? the _____

Questions and Answers

Listen to your teacher.
Then take turns reading the questions and answers.

1. Is Lucas a girl?   No, he isn't.

2. Is Lucas 10 years old?   No, he isn't.

3. Is Lucas from Brazil?   Yes, he is.

4. Is Lucas in the United States?   Yes, he is.

5. Does Lucas speak Spanish?   Yes, he does.

6. Does Lucas speak English?   Yes, he does.

7. Is Lucas a translator?   Yes, he is.

Circle Yes or No

1. Lucas lives in Florida.		Yes	No
2. Lucas's father speaks English.		Yes	No
3. Lucas's father has a carpet business.		Yes	No
4. Lucas makes phone calls for his teacher.		Yes	No
5. Lucas fills in forms at the hospital.		Yes	No
6. Lucas's brother wants a job.		Yes	No
7. Lucas's sister reads English.		Yes	No
8. Lucas helps his father buy a car.		Yes	No
9. Lucas helps new kids at school.		Yes	No
10. Lucas likes the United States.		Yes	No

What Happened First?

What happened first? Write 1 on the line.
What happened second? Write 2 on the line.

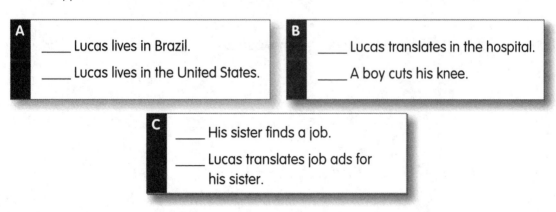

A
_____ Lucas lives in Brazil.
_____ Lucas lives in the United States.

B
_____ Lucas translates in the hospital.
_____ A boy cuts his knee.

C
_____ His sister finds a job.
_____ Lucas translates job ads for his sister.

Working with Words

Put the Words in the Spaces

fills in   helps   speaks   cuts   makes   finds   buys

1. Lucas _____ English.

2. Lucas _____ phone calls.

3. A boy _____ his knee.

4. Lucas _____ forms.

5. Lucas's sister _____ a job.

6. A woman _____ a car.

7. Lucas _____ new kids at school.

Act It Out

Listen to your teacher.
Act out the word.

phone   cut   knee   read   newspaper   car   doctor   friend

Matching Sentences with Pictures

What is in the picture?
Write the sentences beside the pictures.

He makes phone calls for his father.

He helps a woman buy a car.

He fills in forms at the hospital.

For Lucas, helping people is fun!

Lucas speaks Spanish, Portuguese, and English.

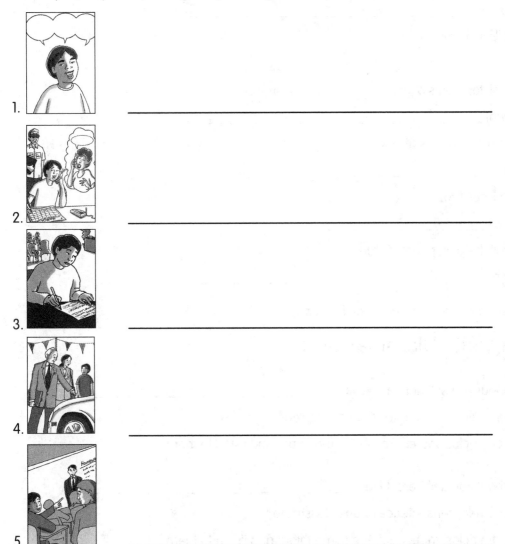

1. _____

2. _____

3. _____

4. _____

5. _____

About Me

Writing About Myself

Listen to your teacher read the sentences.
Repeat the sentences.
Write about yourself in the blanks.

1. Lucas speaks Spanish, Portuguese, and English.

    I speak _____.

2. Lucas fills in forms.

    I _____.

3. Lucas's sister wants a job.

    I want _____.

4. Lucas helps new kids at school.

    I help _____.

5. Lucas misses Brazil.

    I miss _____.

6. For Lucas, helping people is fun!

    For me, _____!

Read the sentences and your answers to a partner.

Talking with Classmates

1. Write about yourself here: **I speak** _____.

2. Stand up. Tell your sentence to one classmate.

3. Talk to other classmates. Say the same thing, and listen to them.

4. Write about yourself here: **I like** _____.

5. Stand up. Tell your sentence to one classmate.

6. Talk to other classmates. Say the same thing, and listen to them.

Lucas Silva _____ in Georgia.

He is twelve years old.

He _____ from Brazil.

He speaks Spanish, Portuguese, _____ English.

His family and friends speak Spanish

_____ Portuguese.

But they don't speak English.

Lucas's father has a carpet business.

Lucas makes _____ calls for his father.

A boy cuts his _____.

Lucas fills in forms at the hospital.

He _____ for the family.

Lucas's sister wants a job.

He translates _____ ads for her.

His sister finds a job.

Lucas _____ a woman buy a car.

He helps new kids _____ school.

Lucas misses Brazil.

But he likes the United _____.

For Lucas, helping people is fun!

Look at the story on page 93.
Make corrections.
Then do Story 1B.

Lucas Silva _____ in Georgia.

He is twelve years old.

He _____ from Brazil.

He speaks Spanish, Portuguese, _____ English.

His family and friends speak Spanish

_____ Portuguese.

But they don't speak English.

Lucas's father has a carpet business.

Lucas makes _____ calls for his father.

A boy cuts his _____.

Lucas fills in forms at the hospital.

He _____ for the family.

Lucas's sister wants a job.

He translates _____ ads for her.

His sister finds a job.

Lucas _____ a woman buy a car.

He helps new kids _____ school.

Lucas misses Brazil.

But he likes the United _____.

For Lucas, helping people is fun!

Look at the story on page 93.
Make corrections.
Then do Story 2A.

Lucas Silva _____ _____ Georgia.

He is twelve years old.

_____ is from Brazil.

He speaks Spanish, Portuguese, and _____.

His family and _____ speak Spanish

or Portuguese.

But they don't _____ English.

Lucas's father has a carpet _____.

Lucas makes phone calls for his _____.

A boy cuts his knee.

Lucas _____ _____ forms

at the hospital.

He translates _____ the family.

Lucas's sister wants a _____.

He translates job ads for her.

His _____ finds a job.

Lucas helps a woman _____ a car.

He helps new kids at _____.

Lucas misses Brazil.

But he _____ the United States.

For Lucas, helping people is fun!

Look at the story on page 93.
Make corrections.
Then do Story 2B.

Fill in the Blanks

Lucas Silva _____ _____ Georgia.

He is twelve years old.

_____ is from Brazil.

He speaks Spanish, Portuguese, and _____.

His family and _____ speak Spanish

or Portuguese.

But they don't _____ English.

Lucas's father has a carpet _____.

Lucas makes phone calls for his _____.

A boy cuts his knee.

Lucas _____ _____ forms

at the hospital.

He translates _____ the family.

Lucas's sister wants a _____.

He translates job ads for her.

His _____ finds a job.

Lucas helps a woman _____ a car.

He helps new kids at _____.

Lucas misses Brazil.

But he _____ the United States.

For Lucas, helping people is fun!

Look at the story on page 93.
Make corrections.
Then do Story 3A.

_____ Silva lives in Georgia.

_____ is twelve _____ old.

He is _____ Brazil.

He speaks Spanish, Portuguese, _____ English.

His family _____ _____ speak

Spanish or Portuguese.

_____ they don't _____ _____.

Lucas's father _____ a carpet _____.

Lucas makes _____ _____ for his father.

A boy _____ his knee.

Lucas fills in forms at _____ _____.

He translates for _____ _____.

Lucas's _____ wants a _____.

_____ _____ job ads for her.

His sister _____ a job.

Lucas helps a woman _____ _____

_____.

He _____ new kids at school.

Lucas _____ Brazil.

_____ he likes the United States.

For Lucas, helping _____ is fun!

Look at the story on page 93.
Make corrections.
Then do Story 3B.

Fill in the Blanks

_____ Silva lives in Georgia.

_____ is twelve _____ old.

He is _____ Brazil.

He speaks Spanish, Portuguese, _____ English.

His family _____ _____ speak

Spanish or Portuguese.

_____ they don't _____ _____.

Lucas's father _____ a carpet _____.

Lucas makes _____ _____ for his father.

A boy _____ his knee.

Lucas fills in forms at _____ _____.

He translates for _____ _____.

Lucas's _____ wants a _____.

_____ _____ job ads for her.

His sister _____ a job.

Lucas helps a woman _____ _____

_____.

He _____ new kids at school.

Lucas _____ Brazil.

_____ he likes the United States.

For Lucas, helping _____ is fun!

Look at the story on page 93.
Make corrections.

The Big Picture

1. What is in the picture? Tell a partner.
2. Tell your teacher the words.
3. Say the words your teacher writes on the board.
4. Write the words on your picture.
5. Look at your partner's book. Are the words in the right places?

Reading

Living in the Library

Teaching suggestions on page 137.

1. Steven is a student at New York University.

2. He is poor.

3. He pays for university tuition.

4. He pays for books.

5. Rent in New York City is very expensive.

6. So Steven lives in the university library.

7. He sleeps on four chairs
   in the library.

8. He washes his clothes in
   the library bathroom.

9. He eats crackers and drinks
   orange juice.

10. Steven is a good student
    and a good writer.

11. He knows many things
    about life.

12. On the Internet, Steven
    writes about his life.

13. Many people read about Steven's life.

14. Many people help him.

15. The university finds a room for him.

16. Steven likes his new life.

Write the Words You Hear

Your teacher will choose six words or phrases from the story.
Listen to your teacher.
Repeat the word.
Write the word.

1. _____

2. _____

3. _____

4. _____

5. _____

6. _____

Reading without Pictures

Teaching suggestions on page 137.

Living in the Library

Steven is a student at New York University.
He is poor.
He pays for university tuition.
He pays for books.
Rent in New York City is very expensive.
So Steven lives in the university library.
He sleeps on four chairs in the library.
He washes his clothes in the library bathroom.
He eats crackers and drinks orange juice.
Steven is a good student and a good writer.
He knows many things about life.
On the Internet, Steven writes about his life.
Many people read about Steven's life.
Many people help him.
The university finds a room for him.
Steven likes his new life.

Understanding the Story

Find the Answer

1. Where does Steven live? in the _____

2. Where does Steven sleep? on four _____

3. What does Steven drink? _____

4. What does Steven write? about his _____

5. Who helps Steven? many _____

Questions and Answers

Listen to your teacher.
Then take turns reading the questions and answers.

1. Is Steven a teacher?   No, he isn't.

2. Are books expensive?   Yes, they are.

3. Is rent expensive in New York City?   Yes, it is.

4. Is Steven poor?   Yes, he is.

5. Is Steven a good student?   Yes, he is.

6. Is Steven a good writer?   Yes, he is.

Circle Yes or No

1. Steven is a student in high school.	Yes	No
2. Steven is poor.	Yes	No
3. Steven pays for books.	Yes	No
4. Steven lives in the university library.	Yes	No
5. Steven has a home.	Yes	No
6. Steven sleeps in a bed in the library.	Yes	No
7. Steven is a good student.	Yes	No
8. Steven is a bad writer.	Yes	No
9. Many people help Steven.	Yes	No
10. Steven likes his new life.	Yes	No

What Happened First?

What happened first? Write 1 on the line.
What happened second? Write 2 on the line.

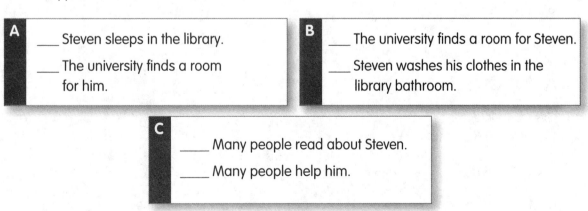

A
___ Steven sleeps in the library.
___ The university finds a room for him.

B
___ The university finds a room for Steven.
___ Steven washes his clothes in the library bathroom.

C
___ Many people read about Steven.
___ Many people help him.

Working with Words

Listen, Repeat, and Write

Listen to your teacher say the words.
Repeat each word.
Spell each word.
Write the missing letters.
Then write the words.

poor	university	books	sleeps	keeps
washes	eats	drinks	learns	people

1. p __ __ r   _____

2. u n __ v __ r s __ t y   _____

3. b __ __ k s   _____

4. s l __ __ p s   _____

5. k __ __ p s   _____

6. w __ s h __ s   _____

7. e a __ __   _____

8. d __ __ n __ s   _____

9. l e a __ __ __ __   _____

10. p __ __ p l e   _____

Act It Out

Listen to your teacher.
Act out the word.

sleep	wash	take a shower	book	drink
read	write	eat	chair	clothes

Matching Sentences with Pictures

What is in the picture?
Write the sentences beside the pictures.

Steven washes his clothes in the library bathroom.

On the Internet, he writes about his life.

Rent in New York City is very expensive.

Steven is poor.

The university finds a room for him.

1. _____

2. _____

3. _____

4. _____

5. _____

About Me

Writing About Myself

Listen to your teacher read the sentences.
Repeat the sentences.
Write about yourself in the blanks.

1. Steven is a student at New York University.

    I am a student at _____.

2. Steven pays for books.

    I pay for _____.

3. Steven drinks orange juice.

    I drink _____.

4. Steven eats crackers.

    I eat _____.

5. Steven washes his clothes in the library bathroom.

    I wash my clothes _____.

6. Steven is a good writer.

    I am a good _____.

Read the sentences and your answers to a partner.

Talking with Classmates

1. Write about yourself here: **I eat** _____.

2. Stand up. Tell your sentence to one classmate.

3. Talk to other classmates. Say the same thing, and listen to them.

4. Write about yourself here: **I live** _____.

5. Stand up. Tell your sentence to one classmate.

6. Talk to other classmates. Say the same thing, and listen to them.

Steven is a _____ at New York University.

He is poor.

He _____ for university tuition.

He pays for books.

Rent in _____ York City is very expensive.

So Steven lives in the university _____.

He sleeps on four chairs in the library.

He _____ his clothes in the library bathroom.

He eats crackers and _____ orange juice.

Steven is a good student and a good _____.

He knows many things about life.

On the Internet, Steven _____ about his life.

Many people read _____ Steven's life.

Many people help him.

The university finds _____ room for him.

Steven likes his new life.

Look at the story on page 109.
Make corrections.
Then do Story 1B.

Fill in the Blanks

Steven is a _____ at New York University.

He is poor.

He _____ for university tuition.

He pays for books.

Rent in _____ York City is very expensive.

So Steven lives in the university _____.

He sleeps on four chairs in the library.

He _____ his clothes in the library bathroom.

He eats crackers and _____ orange juice.

Steven is a good student and a good _____.

He knows many things about life.

On the Internet, Steven _____ about his life.

Many people read _____ Steven's life.

Many people help him.

The university finds _____ room for him.

Steven likes his new life.

Look at the story on page 109.
Make corrections.
Then do Story 2A.

Steven _____ a student at New York University.

_____ is poor.

He pays for _____ tuition.

He pays for books.

_____ in New York City is very _____.

So Steven lives _____ the university library.

He sleeps on _____ chairs in the library.

He washes his _____ in the library bathroom.

He _____ crackers and drinks orange juice.

Steven _____ a good student and

a _____ writer.

He knows many things about _____.

On the Internet, Steven writes _____ his life.

Many _____ read about Steven's life.

Many people _____ him.

The university finds a room _____ him.

Steven likes his _____ life.

Look at the story on page 109.
Make corrections.
Then do Story 2B.

Steven _____ a student at New York University.

_____ is poor.

He pays for _____ tuition.

He pays for books.

_____ in New York City is very _____.

So Steven lives _____ the university library.

He sleeps on _____ chairs in the library.

He washes his _____ in the library bathroom.

He _____ crackers and drinks orange juice.

Steven _____ a good student and

a _____ writer.

He knows many things about _____.

On the Internet, Steven writes _____ his life.

Many _____ read about Steven's life.

Many people _____ him.

The university finds a room _____ him.

Steven likes his _____ life.

Look at the story on page 109.
Make corrections.
Then do Story 3A.

Steven is _____ student at

New York _____.

He is poor.

_____ _____ for university tuition.

He pays _____ books.

Rent _____ New York City is

_____ expensive.

So Steven _____ _____ the university library.

_____ _____ on four chairs in

_____ library.

He _____ his clothes in the library _____.

He eats crackers and _____ orange _____.

Steven is a _____ _____ and

_____ good writer.

He _____ many _____ about life.

_____ _____ Internet,

Steven _____ about his life.

Many people _____ _____ Steven's life.

_____ people help _____.

The university _____ a room for _____.

Steven _____ his new life.

Look at the story on page 109.
Make corrections.
Then do Story 3B.

3B Fill in the Blanks

Steven is _____ student at

New York _____.

He is poor.

_____ _____ for university tuition.

He pays _____ books.

Rent _____ New York City is

_____ expensive.

So Steven _____ _____ the university library.

_____ _____ on four chairs in

_____ library.

He _____ his clothes in the library _____.

He eats crackers and _____ orange _____.

Steven is a _____ _____ and

_____ good writer.

He _____ many _____ about life.

_____ _____ Internet,

Steven _____ about his life.

Many people _____ _____ Steven's life.

_____ people help _____.

The university _____ a room for _____.

Steven _____ his new life.

Look at the story on page 109.
Make corrections.

The Big Picture

1. What is in the picture? Tell a partner.
2. Tell your teacher the words.
3. Say the words your teacher writes on the board.
4. Write the words on your picture.
5. Look at your partner's book. Are the words in the right places?

Reading

Alex and Beth

Teaching suggestions on page 137.

1. Alex goes to a department store.

2. He wants a beautiful present for his girlfriend.

3. He looks and looks.

4. Beth is a salesclerk in the store.

5. She helps Alex. "Look!" she says. "Here is a nice green sweater!"

6. "Here is a beautiful black dress!"

7. "Here is a lovely yellow blouse!"

8. "Here is a pretty red skirt!"

9. "Here is a very nice blue coat."

10. Alex likes the black dress.

11. Beth puts the dress in a pretty white box.

12. Two weeks later, Alex comes back.

13. He returns the dress.

14. "My girlfriend doesn't like the dress," Alex says.

15. "She has another boyfriend."

16. Beth looks at Alex and smiles. "My name is Beth," she says.

Write the Words You Hear

Your teacher will choose six words or phrases from the story.
Listen to your teacher.
Repeat the word.
Write the word.

1. _____

2. _____

3. _____

4. _____

5. _____

6. _____

Reading without Pictures

Teaching suggestions on page 137.

Alex and Beth

Alex goes to a department store.
He wants a beautiful present for his girlfriend.
He looks and looks.
Beth is a salesclerk in the store.
She helps Alex. "Look!" she says. "Here is a nice green sweater!"
"Here is a beautiful black dress!"
"Here is a lovely yellow blouse!"
"Here is a pretty red skirt!"
"Here is a very nice blue coat."
Alex likes the black dress.
Beth puts the dress in a pretty white box.
Two weeks later, Alex comes back.
He returns the dress.
"My girlfriend doesn't like the dress," Alex says.
"She has another boyfriend."
Beth looks at Alex and smiles. "My name is Beth," she says.

Understanding the Story

Find the Answer

1. Where does Alex go? to a _____

2. What does Alex want to buy? a _____ for his _____

3. Who is Beth? a _____

4. What does Alex like? the black _____

5. What does Alex return? the _____

Questions and Answers

Listen to your teacher.
Then take turns reading the questions and answers.

1. Is Beth a salesclerk?   Yes, she is.

2. Is the dress black?   Yes, it is.

3. Is the blouse green?   No, it isn't.

4. Is the coat blue?   Yes, it is.

5. Is the black dress beautiful?   Yes, it is.

6. Is the black dress ugly?   No, it isn't.

7. Is the dress in a white box?   Yes, it is.

8. Is Beth Alex's girlfriend?   No, she isn't.

Circle Yes or No

1. Alex goes to a bookstore.   Yes   No
2. Alex wants a beautiful present for his girlfriend.   Yes   No
3. Beth is a salesclerk in the store.   Yes   No
4. Beth says, "Here is a beautiful black sweater!"   Yes   No
5. Beth says, "Here is a lovely yellow blouse!"   Yes   No
6. Beth puts the dress in a black box.   Yes   No
7. Three weeks later, Alex comes back.   Yes   No
8. Alex's girlfriend likes the dress.   Yes   No
9. Alex's girlfriend has another boyfriend.   Yes   No
10. Beth says, "I am your girlfriend."   Yes   No

What Happened First?

What happened first? Write 1 on the line.
What happened second? Write 2 on the line.

A
_____ Beth shows Alex a dress and a blouse.

_____ Alex first sees Beth.

B
_____ Alex likes the black dress.

_____ Beth puts the black dress in a box.

C
_____ Alex comes back to the store.

_____ Beth says, "My name is Beth."

Working with Words

Categories

Write the words in the right places.

Alex	sweater	red	skirt	girlfriend	green	dress
Beth	yellow	boyfriend	blue	coat	white	black

People	Clothes	Colors
Alex	sweater	red

Act It Out

Listen to your teacher.
Act out the word.

look	put in a box	dress	sweater	skirt
blouse	coat	money	smile	

Matching Sentences with Pictures

What is in the picture?
Write the sentences beside the pictures.

Alex wants a beautiful present for his girlfriend.   Alex returns the dress.

Beth helps Alex. "Here is a beautiful black dress!"   Beth puts the dress in a pretty white box.

"My girlfriend doesn't like the dress," Alex says.

1. _____

2. _____

3. _____

4. _____

5. _____

About Me

Writing About Myself

Listen to your teacher read the sentences.
Repeat the sentences.
Write about yourself in the blanks.

1. Alex goes to a department store.

    I go to _____.

2. Beth is a salesclerk.

    I am _____.

3. Alex likes the black dress.

    I like _____.

4. Alex buys the black dress.

    I buy _____.

5. Alex has a girlfriend.

    I have _____.

6. Alex's girlfriend doesn't like the dress.

    I don't like _____.

Read the sentences and your answers to a partner.

Talking with Classmates

1. Write about yourself here: **I want** _____.

2. Stand up. Tell your sentence to one classmate.

3. Talk to other classmates. Say the same thing, and listen to them.

4. Write about yourself here: **I don't like** _____.

5. Stand up. Tell your sentence to one classmate.

6. Talk to other classmates. Say the same thing, and listen to them.

Alex _____ to a department store.

He wants a beautiful _____ for his girlfriend.

He looks and looks.

Beth _____ a salesclerk in the store.

She helps Alex. "_____!" she says. "Here is

a nice green sweater!"

"Here _____ a beautiful black dress!"

"Here is a lovely _____ blouse!"

"Here is a pretty red skirt!"

"_____ is a very nice blue _____."

Alex likes the black dress.

Beth puts the _____ in a pretty white box.

Two weeks later, Alex _____ back.

He returns the dress.

"My girlfriend doesn't _____ the dress,"

Alex says.

"She has another boyfriend."

Beth looks _____ Alex and smiles.

"My name is Beth," she says.

Look at the story on page 125.
Make corrections.
Then do Story 1B.

Fill in the Blanks

Alex _____ to a department store.

He wants a beautiful _____ for his girlfriend.

He looks and looks.

Beth _____ a salesclerk in the store.

She helps Alex. "_____!" she says. "Here is

a nice green sweater!"

"Here _____ a beautiful black dress!"

"Here is a lovely _____ blouse!"

"Here is a pretty red skirt!"

"_____ is a very nice blue _____."

Alex likes the black dress.

Beth puts the _____ in a pretty white box.

Two weeks later, Alex _____ back.

He returns the dress.

"My girlfriend doesn't _____ the dress,"

Alex says.

"She has another boyfriend."

Beth looks _____ Alex and smiles.

"My name is Beth," she says.

Look at the story on page 125.
Make corrections.
Then do Story 2A.

Alex goes to a department _____.

He wants a beautiful present for his _____.

He looks and looks.

Beth is a _____ in the store.

She _____ Alex. "Look!" she says. "Here is a

_____ green sweater!"

"Here is a beautiful _____ dress!"

"Here is a lovely yellow _____!"

"Here is a pretty red skirt!"

"_____ is a very nice blue coat."

Alex _____ the black dress.

Beth _____ the dress in a pretty white

_____.

Two weeks later, Alex comes back.

He _____ the dress.

"My girlfriend doesn't like _____

_____," Alex says.

"She has another boyfriend."

Beth _____ at Alex and smiles.

"My name _____ Beth," she says.

Look at the story on page 125.
Make corrections.
Then do Story 2B.

Fill in the Blanks

Alex goes to a department _____.

He wants a beautiful present for his _____.

He looks and looks.

Beth is a _____ in the store.

She _____ Alex. "Look!" she says. "Here is a

_____ green sweater!"

"Here is a beautiful _____ dress!"

"Here is a lovely yellow _____!"

"Here is a pretty red skirt!"

"_____ is a very nice blue coat."

Alex _____ the black dress.

Beth _____ the dress in a pretty white

_____.

Two weeks later, Alex comes back.

He _____ the dress.

"My girlfriend doesn't like _____

_____," Alex says.

"She has another boyfriend."

Beth _____ at Alex and smiles.

"My name _____ Beth," she says.

Look at the story on page 125.
Make corrections.
Then do Story 3A.

Alex goes _____ a department _____.

He _____ a beautiful _____

for his girlfriend.

He looks _____ _____.

Beth is a salesclerk _____ _____

_____.

She helps Alex. "Look!" _____ says, "Here is a

_____ green sweater!"

"_____ _____ a beautiful black dress!"

"Here is a lovely yellow _____!"

"Here is a _____ red skirt!"

"Here is a very nice blue coat."

_____ _____ the black dress.

Beth _____ _____ _____

in a pretty white _____.

_____ weeks later, Alex comes _____.

_____ returns the _____.

"My _____ doesn't _____ the dress,"

Alex says.

"_____ _____ another boyfriend."

Beth _____ _____ Alex and

_____. "My name is Beth," _____ says.

Look at the story on page 125.
Make corrections.
Then do Story 3B.

Alex goes _____ a department _____.

He _____ a beautiful _____

for his girlfriend.

He looks _____ _____.

Beth is a salesclerk _____ _____

_____.

She helps Alex. "Look!" _____ says. "Here is a

_____ green sweater!"

"_____ _____ a beautiful black dress!"

"Here is a lovely yellow _____!"

"Here is a _____ red skirt!"

"Here is a very nice blue coat."

_____ _____ the black dress.

Beth _____ _____ _____

in a pretty white _____.

_____ weeks later, Alex comes _____.

_____ returns the _____.

"My _____ doesn't _____ the dress,"

Alex says.

"_____ _____ another boyfriend."

Beth _____ _____ Alex and

_____. "My name is Beth," _____ says.

Look at the story on page 125.
Make corrections.

Notes to the Teacher

THE EXERCISES

The exercises in *Wow! Stories From Real Life* offer a rich variety of "best practices." Some exercises give students repeated **pattern practice** in varied and engaging ways. Others are **open-ended**, promoting self-expression and real communication with plenty of support from model sentences and pictures. In many of the exercises, students can work on their own without the teacher's direct instruction. We've used an *On Our Own!* icon in these teaching notes to indicate such steps. Our "menu" of exercises and teaching suggestions offers more choices than any single class will need. Play with them and use them as you please!

BOARD WORK

We recommend doing plenty of board work with low-beginning classes. Board work focuses the entire class's attention. Students benefit by:
- seeing things being spelled,
- re-reading words and sentences, and
- correcting their work.

Note: As they are able, have students do the board writing.

Exercise Guidelines: Reading

The Big Picture

> **AT-A-GLANCE STEPS**
> 1. Students tell words to each other.
> 2. Students tell words to you.
> 3. Write words on board; students repeat.
> 4. Students copy words onto their own Big Picture.
> 5. Pairs tell words to each other.
> 6. Erase words; students spell them; write them back up.

FULL DESCRIPTION OF STEPS

1. Each student tells a partner some things they see in The Big Picture in their books. *On Our Own!*
2. Students, as a class, tell you what they see in the picture.
3. Write these words on the board, making sure that meanings are clear. Add more words if you wish.
   As you write each word, say it and ask the class to repeat it.
   Point to each word in the list, say it again, and ask students to repeat.
   Who repeats the words after you? Here are a few options:
   - the whole class;
   - half the class at a time, so students alternate: they sometimes speak and sometimes listen, read, and think;
   - individual rows or groups of students;
   - women, then men (and vice-versa); or
   - pair-share: point to a word; pairs say it to each other.

4. Individually, students copy the words from the board onto The Big Picture in their books, making a personal 'picture dictionary'. **On Our Own!**
5. In pairs, students take turns reading their 'Big Picture' words to each other. **On Our Own!**
6. Erase the words from the board. Then say a word. In unison, students spell out the word you said as you write it back up on the board.

Reading with Pictures

STUDENTS LOOK IT OVER **On Our Own!**

Give students time to study the pictures in the illustrated story and get a general idea of the story.

READ ALOUD; STUDENTS TOUCH PICTURES

1. Read through the entire story aloud, one caption at a time. Ask students to *touch each picture* in their books as you do this.
2. Explain or demonstrate key vocabulary as needed.
3. Ask the class if they would like you to read the story more than once.

READ ALOUD; STUDENTS REPEAT EACH CAPTION

Also referred to as "echo reading," in this activity, read each caption aloud and have students repeat it in unison after you.

MY TURN/YOUR TURN CHORAL READING

Read a caption. Students take turns reading the next caption. *Who gets the next turn?* Perhaps the next table, or row, or students wearing blue, etc.

POPCORN READING **On Our Own!**

A student stands and reads out one caption. This student calls on a classmate to stand up and read the caption after it; the first student sits back down.

READ KEY WORDS; STUDENTS POINT TO THEM

Read aloud a key word from the picture captions. Students find the word in their books and point to it. Encourage students to see where their classmates point.

READ KEY WORDS; STUDENTS CIRCLE THEM

1. Read aloud a key word from the picture captions. Students find the word in their books and circle it. Repeat this with each word.
2. In pairs, students look at what they just circled and take turns reading it to each other. **On Our Own!**
   - They may read just the circled word or phrase, or
     - they may read the whole sentence that contains the circled word or phrase.

Note: You might choose either "Read Key Words; Students Point to Them" or "Read Key Words; Students Circle Them," rather than doing both.

FIND THE PICTURE

Note 1: Try this as a review after doing the exercise Circle Yes or No.
Note 2: To demonstrate this first, write the words "Find the Picture" on the board. Ask two students to come to the board. Coach one to say, for example, "He pays for books. Find the picture!" Coach the other student to hold up his/her book and point to the correct picture. The same two students switch roles and demonstrate with a different caption.

1. Students cover the captions in their books.
2. Read aloud one caption.

3. Students find the matching picture in their books.
4. Students form pairs and do steps 1-3 with their partners. `On Our Own!`
   Variation: One student at a time goes to the front of the class and reads out a caption. The whole class points to that picture in their books, glancing at neighbors to see if they've chosen the same picture. `On Our Own!`

Reading with Pictures and/or Reading without Pictures
Note: For extra practice and variety, try these!

SILENT READING `On Our Own!`
Students silently read the illustrated story in their books.

PAIR READING `On Our Own!`
Students take turns reading the story aloud to each other, alternating sentences.

SENTENCES WITH MISTAKES
1. Read aloud the illustrated story caption by caption, making a factual mistake in some sentences. As you read, students give a thumbs up for a correct sentence and thumbs down for an incorrect one.
2. Students tell you how to correct the false sentences.

STRIP STORY `On Our Own!`
1. Write each story caption on a small strip of paper. Make one set of captions for each group of students.
2. Students form groups. Give a set of captions to each group of students.
3. Students arrange their captions in the correct order (make sure students have closed their books!).
4. Ask one group to read aloud their completed story to the other groups.

STRIP STORY VARIATION FOR FRIENDLY COMPETITION `On Our Own!`
1. Write each story caption on a strip of paper large enough to be seen at a distance. Make one set of captions for each group of students.
2. Students form groups. Give a set of captions and tape to each group of students.
3. Students arrange their captions in the correct order (make sure students have closed their books!).
4. Students then dash to the wall to tape up their story. The first group to finish correctly wins.
5. Ask the "winning" group to read their complete story to the class.

Write the Words You Hear

DICTATION
1. Choose six useful words or phrases from the illustrated story.
2. Read aloud the word or phrase. Students repeat each word or phrase in unison as you say it.
3. Students write the word or phrase in the blanks provided in their books.
   Note: for very low levels, have students find and copy the words from the illustrated story.

PAIR WORK `On Our Own!`
Do the *Dictation* activity above. Then students form pairs and compare their answers.

COMPREHENSION CHECKS *(Choose A or B)*
A. Give the Answers
   After the *Dictation* activity, read aloud all six answers and write them on the board.
   Alternatively, invite students to come up and write the answers on the board.
   Variation: Random Numbers
      1. After the Dictation activity, erase the answers from the board.
      2. Say a number between one and six.
      *3. Students tell what they wrote in that blank (students can do this in unison as a whole class, in
         groups or pairs, or as individuals).*
B. Students Give the Answers
   Ask one or more students to come to the board. Do the dictation again, having students write their answers
   on the board. The rest of the class checks the answers in their books and offers advice to the board-writers.

Reading without Pictures (see also *Reading with Pictures*)

PREDICTIONS AND OPINIONS
Invite students to talk about the photograph:
Do the people in the photograph look like the people in the drawings?
What happens in this picture?
What happens before this picture?
What happens after this picture?
Who do you think took this picture?
Do you like these people? Why or why not?

SENTENCE MATCH-UP (a mingling activity)
1. Make a set of sentence strips (one strip for each sentence in the story).
2. Cut each sentence strip into two pieces, for example:

   | **She lives in** / **Apartment 1C.** |

3. Make enough sentence halves so that each student gets one half of a sentence.
4. Put the sentence strips into a container.
5. Each student takes a strip from the container.
6. Students stand up and mingle, reading the words on their strip aloud to one classmate after
   another until they find the missing half of their sentence. *On Our Own!*
7. When all sentence halves are matched, each pair of students reads aloud their sentence to the class.
8. Pairs of students arrange themselves in a line to re-create the story.
9. Pairs read aloud their sentences again, re-telling the story in the correct order.

Exercise Guidelines: Understanding the Story

Find the Answer (a scanning activity)

Note: Lowest-level students can do this simple exercise. Even if they don't fully comprehend, they can scan for the one-word answers to these questions.

1. Read aloud each question.
2. Students repeat the question in unison.
3. Students scan the story in their books and write answers in the blanks.
4. Choose a Wrap-Up activity from page 144.

Questions and Answers

LISTENING

Read aloud each question and answer while students listen. Students tell you if they want a question and answer repeated.

STUDENT-TEACHER CHORAL READING

Read aloud the questions; students read the answers in unison (or answer from memory). Switch; students read the questions and you say the answers.

HALF-AND-HALF CHORAL READING

Half the class reads a question; the other half answers it. Switch.

OUT-OF-ORDER PAIR READING `On Our Own!`

Note: Some students may be able to do this with the answers covered.

Students form pairs and read the questions and answers to each other; however, this time they read the questions out of order. The partner says the answer.

READ QUESTIONS OUT OF ORDER; STUDENTS ANSWER

To check comprehension, read aloud the questions, out of order. Students say or write the answers.

Circle Yes or No

1. Read aloud the sentences while students listen.
2. Students work alone, circling *Yes* or *No*. `On Our Own!`
3. Choose a Wrap-Up activity on page 144.

Optional extension: After the wrap-up, students may correct the "no" sentences so they now answer as "yes."

What Happened First?

Note: To demonstrate this first, give students an example from the here and now. You might say and demonstrate, "I sit down. I stand up." Ask a student to come up and do these actions. Then ask, "What happens first? Lisa sits down or Lisa stands up?"

1. Read aloud the sentences in *What Happened First?*
2. Individually, students complete the exercise. `On Our Own!`
3. Choose a Wrap-Up activity on page 144.

Exercise Guidelines: Working with Words

Categories

Note: To demonstrate this first, explain the word "category" by gathering some groups of things that belong in categories; for example: Things to write with, Things to write on, and Things to read. Hold up a group of objects and say, for example: "These are pens and pencils. I write with pens and pencils." Draw a table on the board that resembles the ones in the book. Title your categories: Things I write with; Things I write on; Things I read. Show one of the category graphs in the book and explain the headings.

1. Individually, students put words in the right categories in their books. On Our Own!
2. Choose a Wrap-Up activity from page 144.
3. Students write down other words they know that fit in the categories.

Note: Consider letting students create their own categories for a list of words.

Listen, Repeat, and Write

Note: This is not a dictation, but a copying and spelling exercise. Students must look carefully at how words are formed.

1. Write the word list on the board. Spell aloud the words as you write them.
2. Read aloud the words again. Students repeat each one in unison.
3. Point to a word; students, in rows or groups, read the word in unison. Repeat with other words on the list.
4. Individual students read aloud the words at their own speed, a few times through the list. (Everyone will be reading at once, at different speeds, etc. This is okay—it's a worthwhile hubbub!) On Our Own!
5. Individually, students fill in the blanks in their books with the right letters. On Our Own!
6. Students correct their work. (Choose a Wrap-Up activity from page 144.)
7. Erase the word list from the board; the class calls out each word in unison as you erase it.
8. Recreate the word list on the board; individual students spell out the words while you or a student writes them back up on the board. (Students may do this with their books open or closed.)

Put the Words in the Spaces

1. Read the list of words aloud. Students repeat the words in unison as you read them.
2. Read each sentence aloud. Say "space" where a blank occurs.
3. Students, individually or in pairs, fill in the blanks. On Our Own!
4. Choose a Wrap-Up activity from page 144.

Matching Sentences with Pictures

Note: To demonstrate this first, ask students to look at the first picture. Have students form pairs and talk about everything they see in the picture. Individually, students call out what they see. Write the words on the board as students call them out. Then read all five possible sentences (captions) while students listen. Finally, call on individual students to read aloud all the sentences.

1. As a class, students choose the best sentence (caption) for the first picture.
2. Individually, students write in all the other sentences. On Our Own!
3. Students form pairs and compare their answers. On Our Own!
4. Choose a Wrap-Up activity from page 144.

Act It Out

Note: This activity works best when students' success rate remains around 90%. Don't move on to step 5 (independent pair work) too soon. Recycle words that students know well, adding new words into the mix as students can handle them.

1. Read aloud one of the words in the list and perform the action while students watch and listen.
2. Again read aloud the word and do the action. Students repeat the words and do the action.
3. Say the word but *don't do* the action. Students repeat the word and do the action.
4. Again, say the word but *don't do* the action. This time, call on individual students to repeat the word and do the action.
5. Students form pairs and take turns completing the above steps using different words on the list. On Our Own!

   Optional: One student comes to the front of the class and does the action; the class says the word and does the action again.

Exercise Guidelines: About Me

Writing About Myself On Our Own!

Note: To demonstrate this first, read aloud the sentences and your answers. For example, you might say: "Darwin and Art are twelve years old. I am thirty-five years old." Go through the entire exercise, telling as much as you want to about yourself.

1. Individually, students complete the exercise by writing their answers in the blanks.
2. Students form pairs and tell each other their stories. Alternatively, they may mingle, talking with more than one classmate.
3. Students sit in front of the class and tell their stories.

MY STORY (Optional Writing Extension) On Our Own!

1. Students copy the sentences about themselves onto a blank piece of paper. They may decorate this paper with a picture of themselves, a drawing, and/or a photograph. (This can be done as homework.)
2. Post these papers on the classroom walls. Students walk around, reading one another's stories and writing comments such as: *Very nice!; Very interesting; Good work; I _____ , too!*

MY PARTNER'S STORY (Optional Speaking Extension) On Our Own!

1. Students form pairs and read their sentences to each other.
2. Each pair then joins another pair to form a group of four. Each student re-tells their first partner's story to the rest of the group.

Talking with Classmates (a mingling activity)

Note 1: In this open-ended activity, students answer unfinished questions and then mingle. There is plenty of student-to-student interaction.
Note 2: To demonstrate this first, complete an open-ended sentence for yourself. Then show students how to mingle, talking to one classmate briefly and moving on to another.

1. Students complete the sentences by writing personal answers in their books. On Our Own!
2. Students stand up and mingle, telling each other their sentences. On Our Own!

3. Students regroup as a class; individual students tell the whole class something interesting from the mingle (for example, "Mohamed loves pizza!").
Optional: Students write something they heard while they mingled. On Our Own!

Exercise Guidelines: Fill in the Blanks

Fill in the Blanks (Progressive Cloze)

For more notes on Progressive Cloze, see *Introduction II*, page 6.

Note 1: Students naturally start to fill in the first blanks they see. But they miss contextual clues if they do this. **Be sure to have your students read through each cloze passage—with pencils down—before they start to fill in the blanks.**

Note 2: There are three cloze versions of each story. You might have students tear these out to ensure they can only see one version at a time.

1. The first version, 1A, has (roughly) every tenth word deleted. Students fill in the blanks, then correct their work by looking back at the original story. They then go to the next page and see 1B, a clean copy of the same exercise; 1A, with the same blanks.
2. Students fill in the blanks once again and correct their work. Of course, they should have more correct answers the second time around!
3. Students do the same with 2A, a different cloze version of the story, this time with more words deleted. They fill in these different blanks, then correct their work.
4. Immediately students do 2B, a clean copy of 2A.
5. The third version of the story, 3A, has even more blanks, including some phrases. As before, students fill in what they can and correct their work.
6. Students immediately do 3B.

That's Progressive Cloze! Grammar, spelling, and vocabulary all in one!

Wrap-Ups

Choose among the following 'wrap-ups' to end any of the exercises:

PARTNERS: Each student compares answers with his/her partner.

PAIRS: Students form pairs and compare answers. Then each pair of students joins another pair to reconfirm and discuss their combined answers.

TEAMS: Students form teams and decide on correct answers. Then each team sends a member to write answers on the board. (This provides immediate feedback to the whole class.)

WHOLE CLASS: A student goes to the front of the class and reads aloud his/her set of answers Any student can challenge an answer and, if correct, take over the spotlight to continue reading answers to the class.